FIVE
5 FINGER
PIANO

Disney® TODAY

T0087284

ISBN 978-1-4950-7030-3

DISTRIBUTED BY

HAL•LEONARD®
7777 W. BLUEMOUND RD. P.O. BOX 13819 MILWAUKEE, WI 53213

In Australia Contact:
Hal Leonard Australia Pty. Ltd.
4 Lentara Court
Cheltenham, Victoria, 3192 Australia
Email: ausadmin@halleonard.com.au

Visit Hal Leonard Online at
www.halleonard.com

Almost There

from THE PRINCESS AND THE FROG

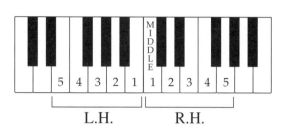

Music and Lyrics by
Randy Newman

I re-mem-ber Dad-dy told me fair-y tales can come true, but you got-ta make 'em hap-pen; it all de-pends on you. So I work real hard each and ev-'ry day. Now

Duet Part (Student plays one octave higher than written.)

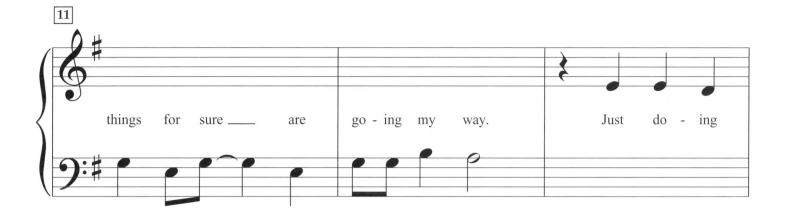

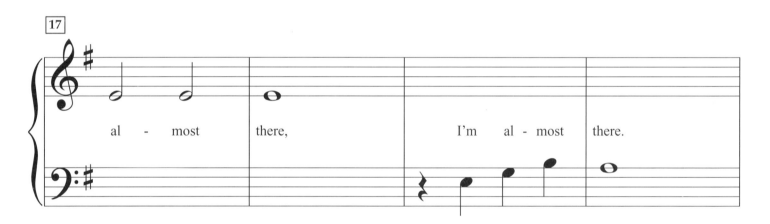

Happy Working Song

from ENCHANTED

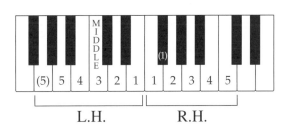

Music by Alan Menken
Lyrics by Stephen Schwartz

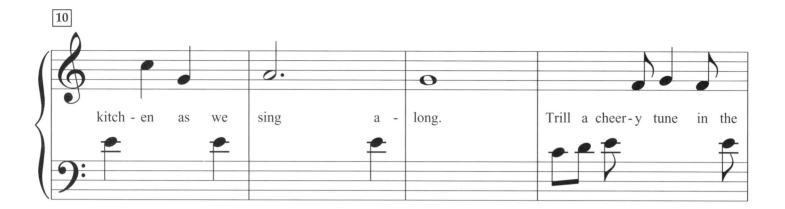

kitch - en as we sing a - long. Trill a cheer - y tune in the

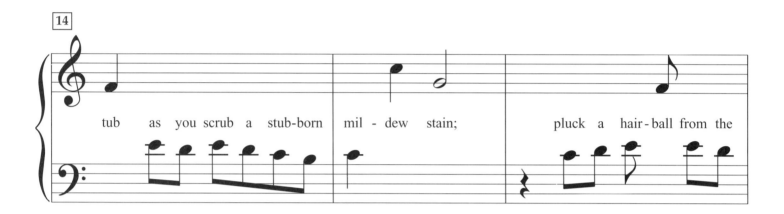

tub as you scrub a stub-born mil - dew stain; pluck a hair-ball from the

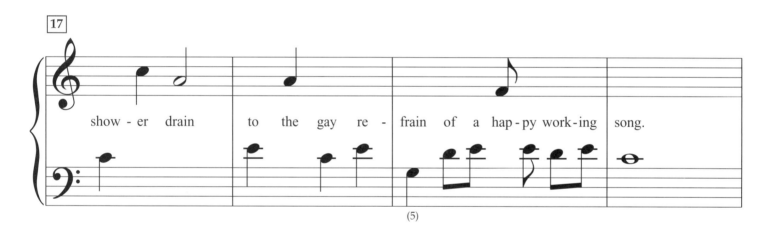

show - er drain to the gay re - frain of a hap - py work - ing song.

(5)

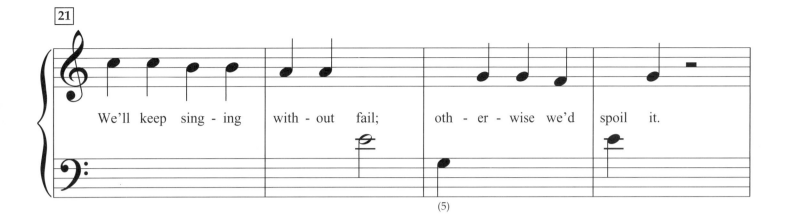

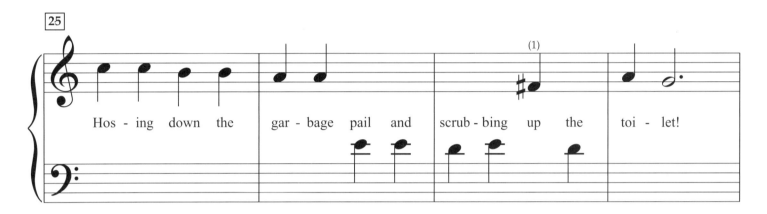

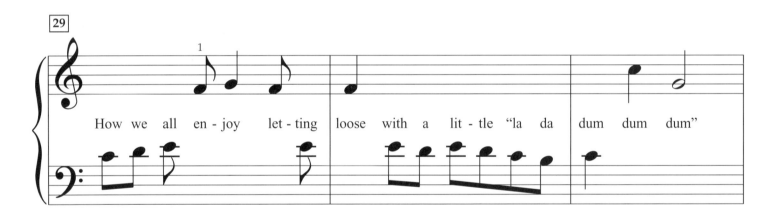

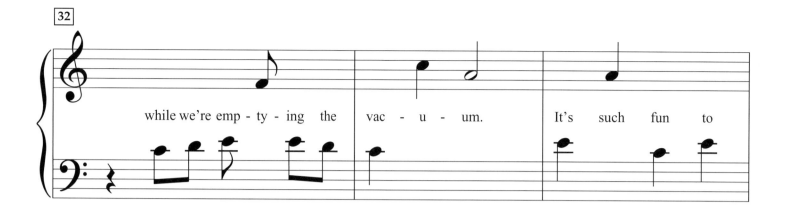

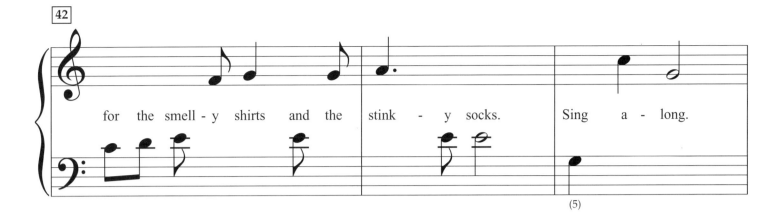

for the smell - y shirts and the stink - y socks. Sing a - long.

(5)

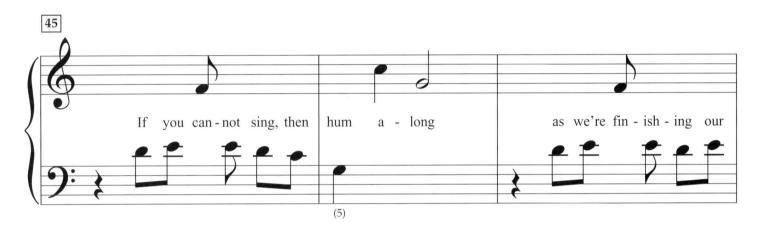

If you can - not sing, then hum a - long as we're fin - ish - ing our

(5)

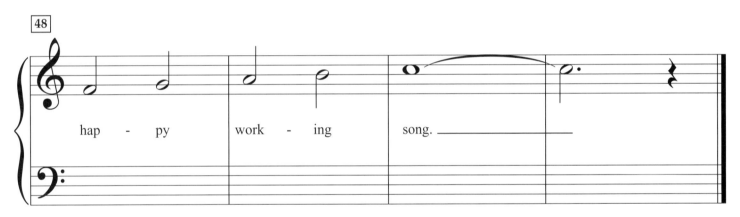

hap - py work - ing song. _____

I See the Light
from TANGLED

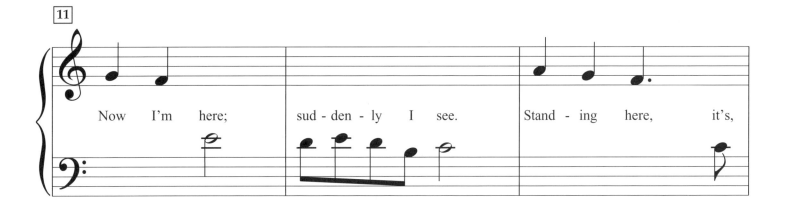

Now I'm here; sud - den - ly I see. Stand - ing here, it's,

oh, so clear I'm where I'm meant to be. And at last I see the

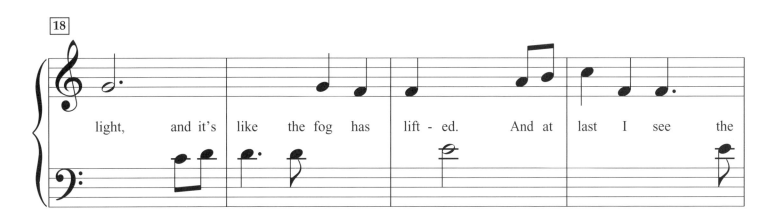

light, and it's like the fog has lift - ed. And at last I see the

light,   and it's   like   the sky   is   new.   And it's   warm   and real   and

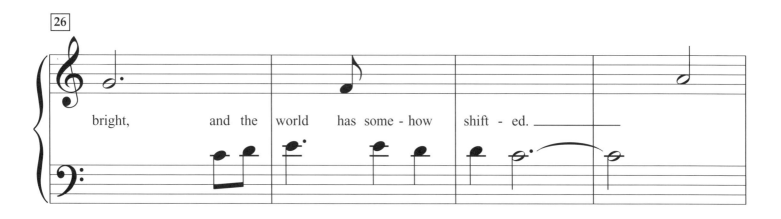

bright,   and the   world   has some - how   shift - ed. _____

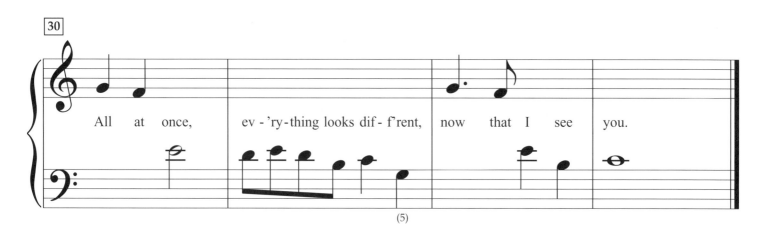

All   at   once,   ev - 'ry-thing looks dif - f'rent,   now   that   I   see   you.

(5)

Let It Go
from FROZEN

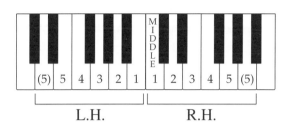

Music and Lyrics by Kristen Anderson-Lopez
and Robert Lopez

Mysterious

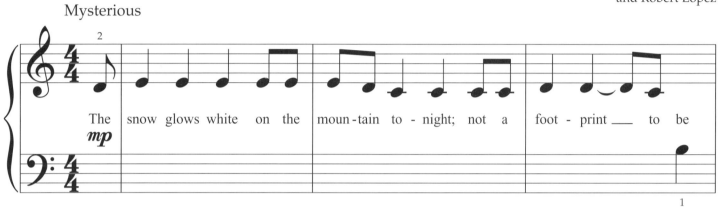

The snow glows white on the moun-tain to-night; not a foot-print ___ to be

seen. A king-dom of i - so - la - tion, and it

Duet Part (Student plays one octave higher than written.)

Mysterious

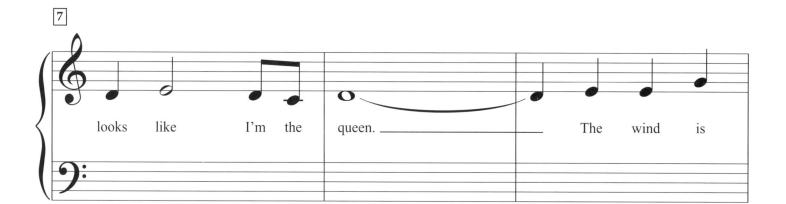

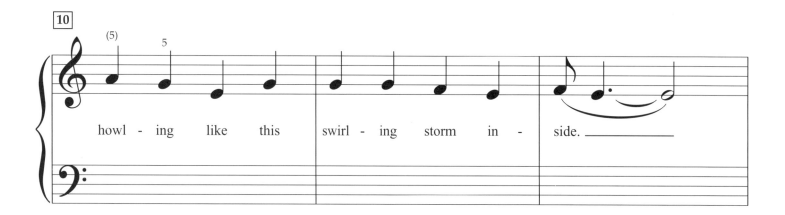

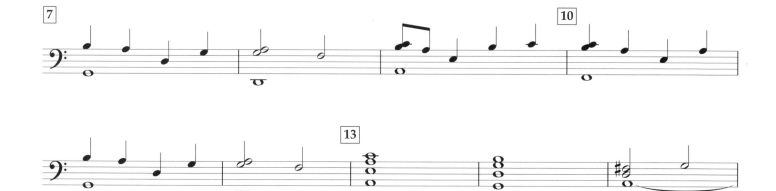

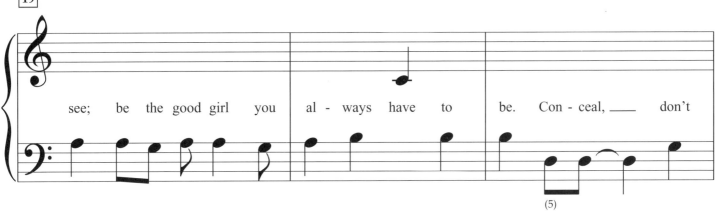

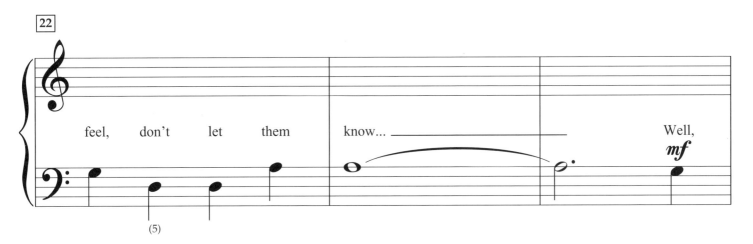

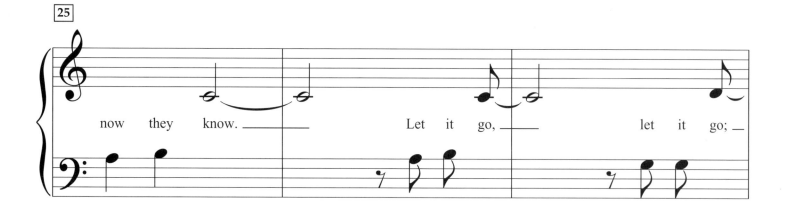

now   they   know. _____   Let   it   go, _____   let   it   go; __

_____   can't   hold   it   back   an - y - more. ____   Let   it   go, __

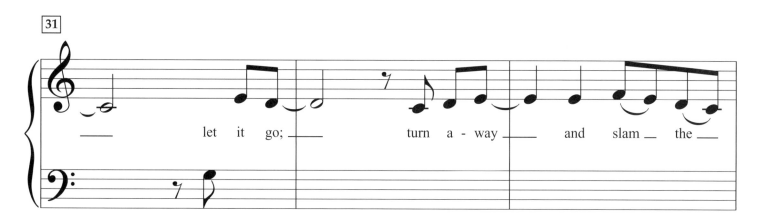

_____   let   it   go; ____   turn   a - way ____   and   slam __ the __

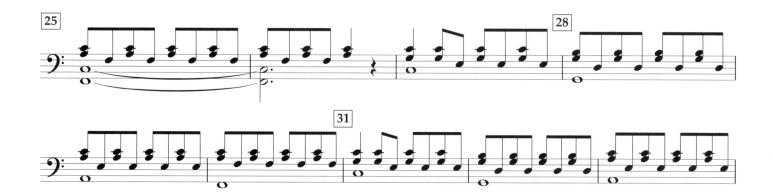

door. _____ I don't care _____ what they're

going to say; _____ let the storm rage on. _____

_____ The cold nev - er both-ered me an - y - way. _____

I've Got a Dream
from TANGLED

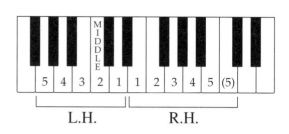

Music by Alan Menken
Lyrics by Glenn Slater

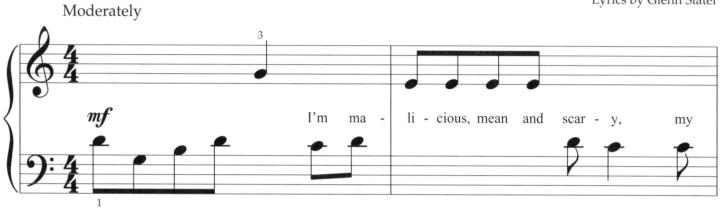

I'm ma - li - cious, mean and scar - y, my

sneer could cur - dle dair - y and vio - lence - wise, my hands are not the

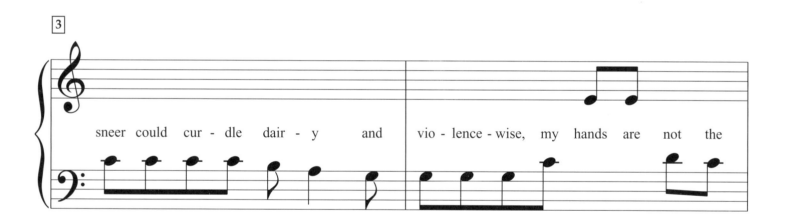

Duet Part (Student plays one octave higher than written.)

Moderately

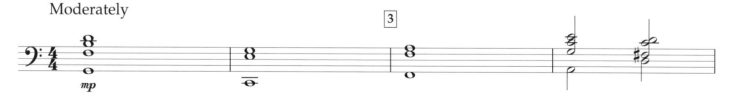

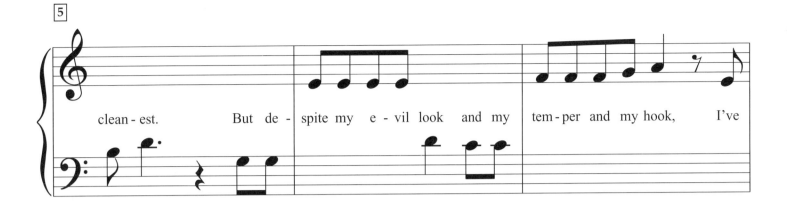

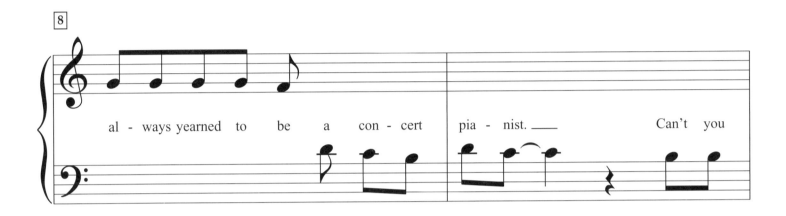

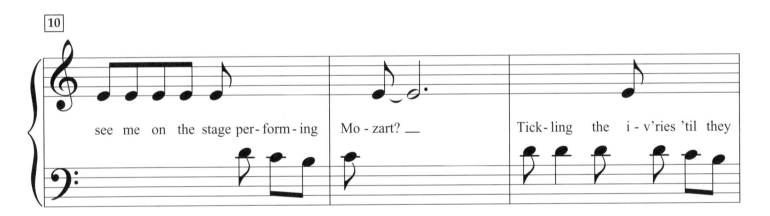

gleam? Yep, I'd rath-er be called dead-ly for my kill-er show-tune med-ley.

Thank you! 'Cause way down deep in-side, I've got a dream. He's got a

dream, he's got a dream. See, I ain't as cruel and vi-cious as I

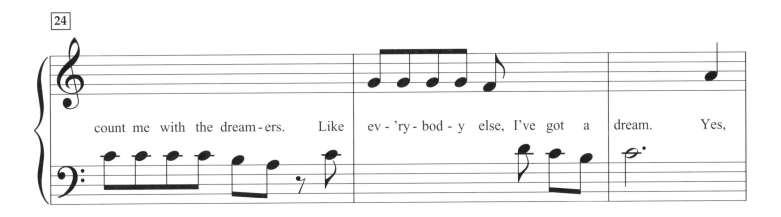

Lava
from LAVA

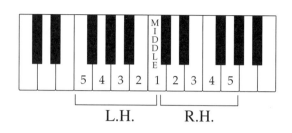

Music and Lyrics by
James Ford Murphy

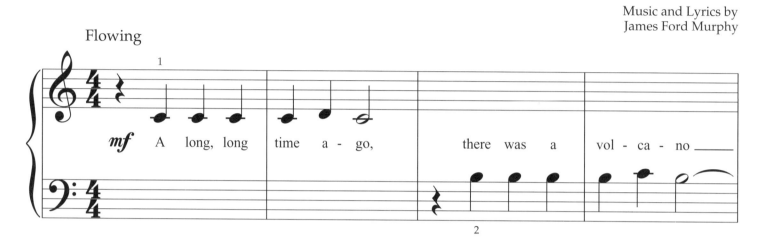

Flowing

mf A long, long time a-go, there was a vol-ca-no

living all a-lone in the mid-dle of the

Duet Part (Student plays one octave higher than written.)

Flowing

mp

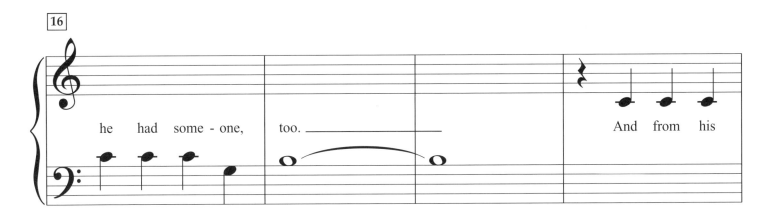

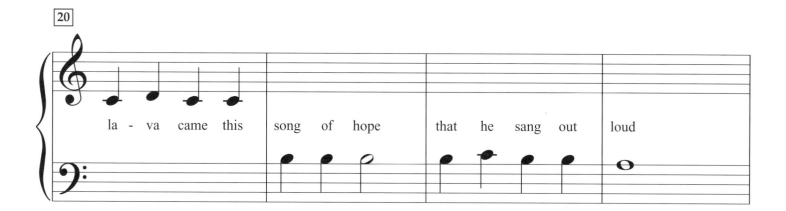

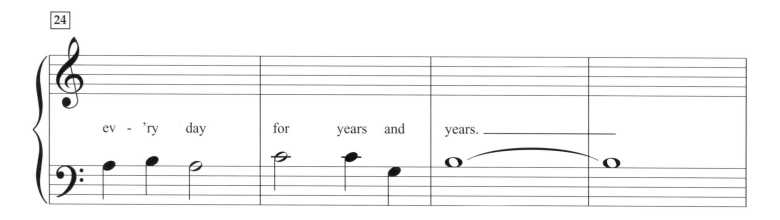

you're   here   with   me   and   I'm   here   with   you.   I

wish   that   the   earth,   sea   and   the   sky   up   a - bove   -   a   will

send   me   some - one   to   la   -   va." _____

True Love's Kiss

from ENCHANTED

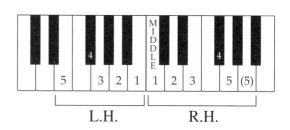

Music by Alan Menken
Lyrics by Stephen Schwartz

I've been dream-ing of a true love's kiss; and a prince I'm hop-ing

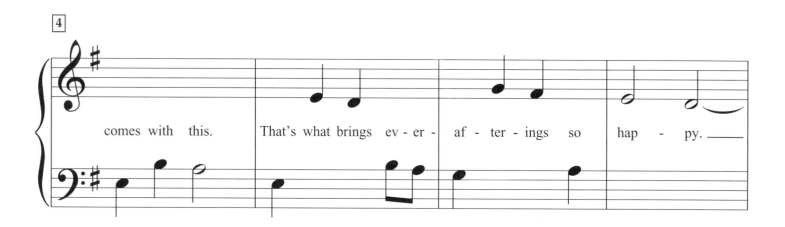

comes with this. That's what brings ev-er- af-ter-ings so hap - py.

Duet Part (Student plays one octave higher than written.)

And that's the rea-son we need lips so much, for lips are the on-ly

things that touch. So, to spend a life of end-less bliss,

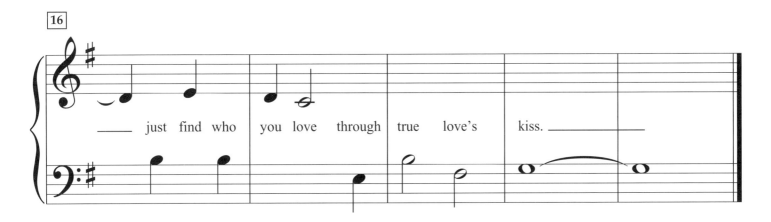

just find who you love through true love's kiss.

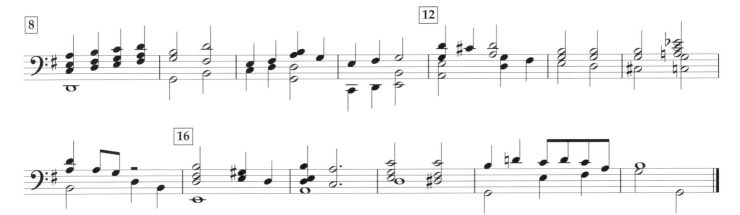

We Belong Together

from TOY STORY 3

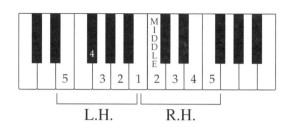

Music and Lyrics by
Randy Newman

With a bounce

mf Don't you turn your back on me; don't you walk _ a - way. _

Don't you tell me that I don't care, 'cause I do. _

Duet Part (Student plays one octave higher than written.)

With a bounce

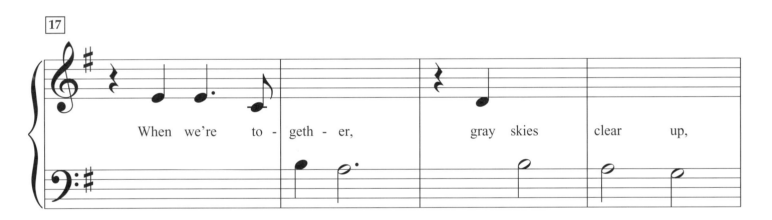

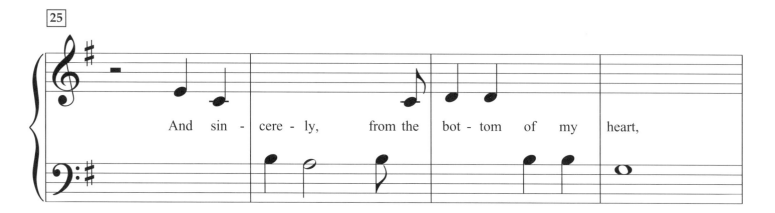

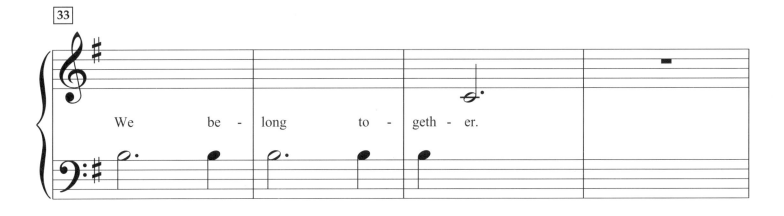

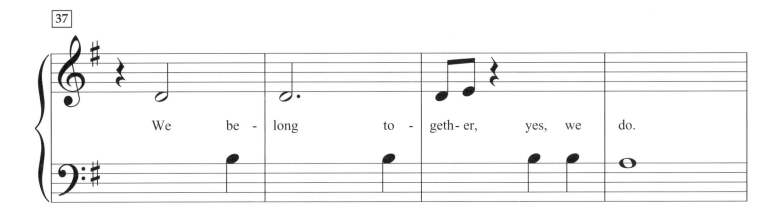

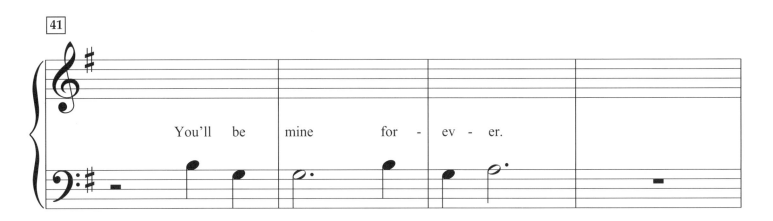

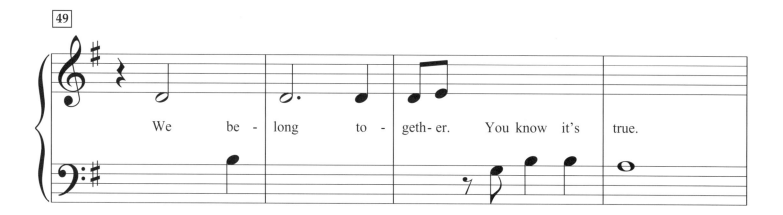

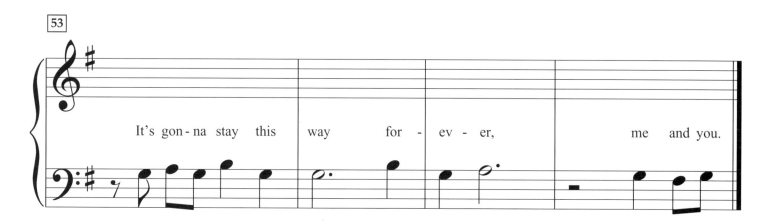